Orcas

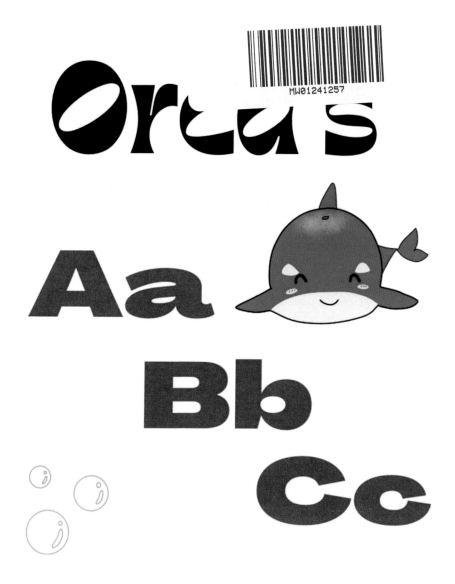

Aa

Bb

Cc

FRIENDS UNDER THE SEA

Written by Kyra
& R.Lloyd

Aa
Anchor

Bb

Boat

Cc

Coral

Dd

Dolphin

Ee

Eel

Ff

Fish

Great
White shark

Hh

Human

Isopod

Jj

Jellyfish

Kk

Kelp

Lobster

Mm

Manatee

Nn

Nurse shark

Oo

Orca

Pp

Plankton

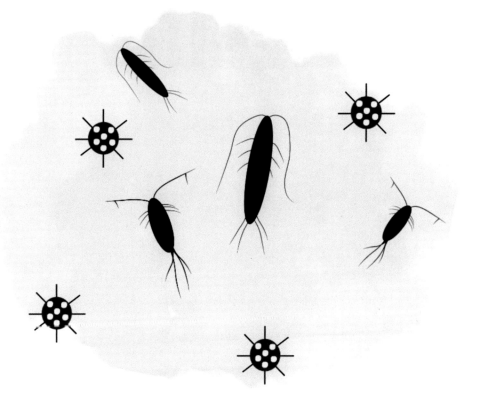

Queen
Angelfish

Ray

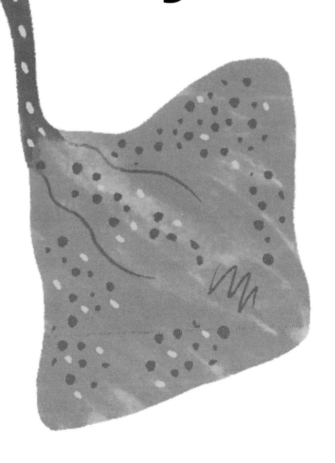

Ss

Starfish

Turtle

Uu

Urchin

Vv

Volcano

Ww

Whale

X-ray fish

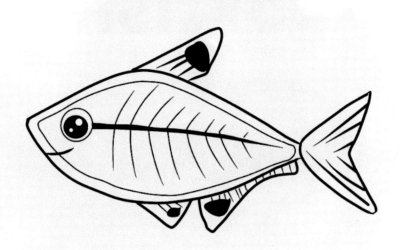

Yy

Yellow
Boxfish

Zz

Zebra fish

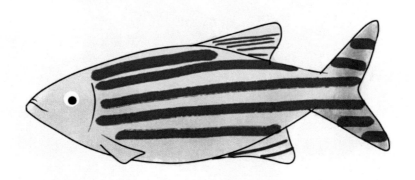

ABCDEFG
HIJKLMNOP
QRSTUVWXYZ

abcdefg
hijklmnop
qrstuvwxyz